THE CHAMELEON KID

Controlling Meltdown Before He Controls You

by

Elaine Marie Larson

Designed by Vivian Strand

AAPC
Autism Asperger Publishing Co.
P.O. Box 23173
Shawnee Mission, Kansas 66283-0173
www.asperger.net

©2008 Autism Asperger Publishing Company
P. O. Box 23173
Shawnee Mission, Kansas 66283-0173
www.asperger.net

Publisher's Cataloging-in-Publication

Larson, Elaine Marie.

   The chameleon kid : controlling meltdown before he controls you /
by Elaine Marie Larson ; illustrated by Vivian Strand. – 1st ed. –
Shawnee Mission, Kan. : Autism Asperger Pub. Co., c2008.

      p. ; cm.
      ISBN: 978-1-934575-22-2
      LCCN: 2008924316

      Summary: An illustrated children's book teaching strategies on
how to avoid having a behavioral meltdown in various situations.
Page spreads show the impending danger of meltdown on the left
and strategies for taming it on the right.
      Includes bibliographical references.

      1. Autistic children – Behavior modification – Juvenile literature.
2. Asperger's syndrome in children – Behavior modification –
Juvenile literature. 3. Anger in children – Juvenile literature.
4. [Autism. 5. Asperger's syndrome.] I. Strand, Vivian. II. Title.

RJ506.A9 L37 2008   2008924316
618.92/85882--dc22   0804

This book is designed in Tekton.

Some illustrations based on photographs from Shutterstock.com.

Printed in the United States of America.

Dedication

This book is dedicated to all children who work hard at becoming Chameleon Kids.

I offer a sincere thank you:

To my daughter-in-law, Jill, who suggested the need for a children's book on meltdowns and fueled my passion for the subject.

To my grandson Sam, for sharing with me the myriad feelings involved with a meltdown.

And to my husband, Norm, for his ongoing encouragement, enthusiasm, and support throughout my writing adventures.

Note to Family, Teachers, and Friends

The Chameleon Kid deals with emotional meltdowns and is written for children with Asperger Syndrome or high-functioning autism. These children often experience emotions such as excitement, anxiety, and anger with greater gusto and staying power than children who do not have an autism spectrum disorder.

The chameleon adapts his color to his surroundings as well as to his mood and communication needs. Similarly, as we learn in this book, the Chameleon Kid can learn to adapt to his surroundings by altering his behavior in dealing with the emotions that precede a meltdown. Through reading about and learning to use positive approaches to handling difficult situations, the child discovers he has the power to eliminate a meltdown, or at the very least lessen its hold on him – just like the Chameleon Kid.

To further support the reader, the book concludes with a checklist of ways to control Meltdown for future use, as well as activities to help the child analyze what feelings or behaviors make Meltdown appear – at school, at home, on the playground, in restaurants, and more.

According to *Asperger Syndrome and Difficult Moments, Practical Solutions for Tantrums, Rage, and Meltdowns* by Brenda Smith Myles and Jack Southwick (2005, Shawnee Mission, KS: Autism Asperger Publishing Company; www.asperger.net), "Our ultimate goal when working with children and youth with AS who experience the rage cycle (Meltdown) is to prevent it from occurring" (p. 38). *The Chameleon Kid* offers suggestions the reader can follow to help him diffuse his emotions before they build up and explode.

For children with Asperger Syndrome and high-functioning autism, controlling their emotions is often challenging, but unquestionably a worthwhile goal. Several other books provide additional guidance for children in learning to deal with their emotions. Suggestions include the following.

When My Worries Get Too Big! gives the young reader relaxation techniques to use when he faces daily challenges (K. D. Buron, 2006. Shawnee Mission, KS: Autism Asperger Publishing Company; www.asperger.net)

A "5" Could Make Me Lose Control, A Hands-On Activity Book introduces a 5-point self-rating system to help children deal with anxious situations (K. D. Buron, 2006. Shawnee Mission, KS: Autism Asperger Publishing Company; www.asperger.net)

My Book Full of Feelings – How to Control and React to the Size of Your Emotions uses an interactive format to help teach children to identify, assess the intensity of, and respond appropriately to their emotions (A. V. Jaffe & K. Gardner, 2006. Shawnee Mission, KS: Autism Asperger Publishing Company; www.asperger.net)

Finally, children on the autism spectrum use direct, precise language and tend to interpret what they hear, see, and read literally. As a result, figurative speech and idioms, which are used in everyday language without much thought, are often confusing to them. In the following pages, I have included some commonly use idioms and their meanings. I hope the reader will find them both interesting and helpful.

E. M. L.

Note to Young Readers

What happens when you get really excited, sad, or worried? Do you use loud or angry words? Are you so mad that you scare those around you? Or maybe you get so frustrated that you shut down and don't talk at all.

Any of these strong feelings may be telling you that Meltdown wants to take over.

Take a cue from the chameleon. If he wants to show his mood or communicate with other chameleons, he changes color. Be a Chameleon Kid! You can make changes in yourself, too, when your emotions are growing too strong. You can learn how to show others your feelings in more positive and non-scary ways. When you practice the ideas in *The Chameleon Kid*, you can control Meltdown before he takes control of you.

As you read this book by yourself, or with an adult, notice how the big and scary Meltdown on the left-hand pages becomes smaller on the right-hand pages when the Chameleon Kid fights back in many different ways. After you have read the book, think about how you can become a Chameleon Kid yourself by doing the activities at the back of the book.

Good luck!

E. M. L.

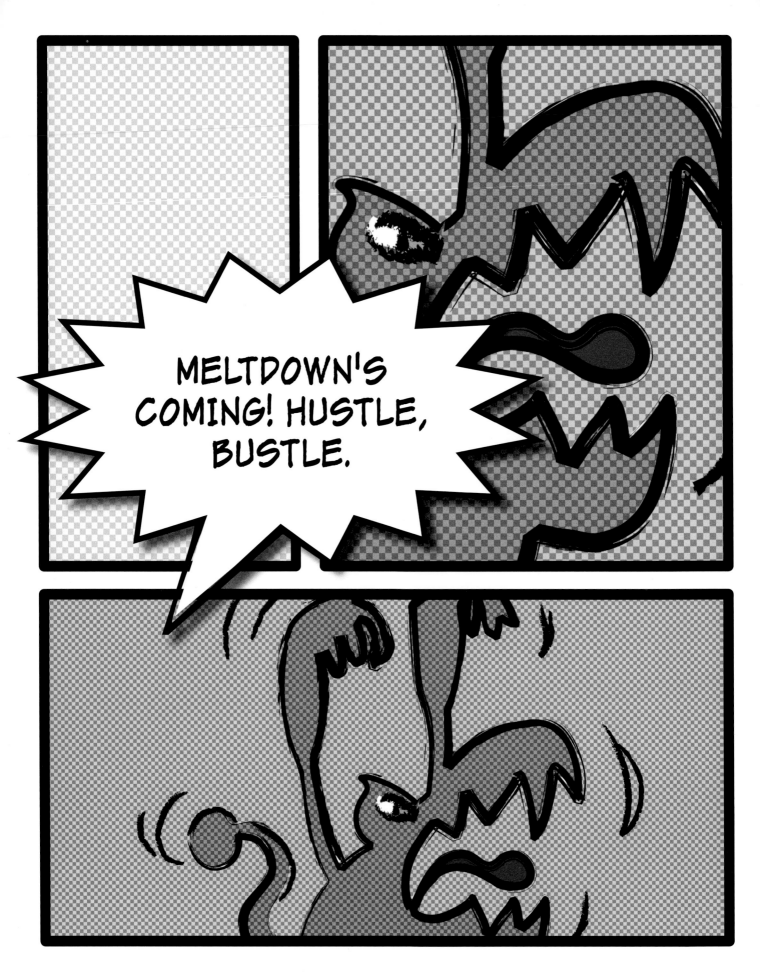

SCREAM IS GROWING, WANTS OUT NOW.

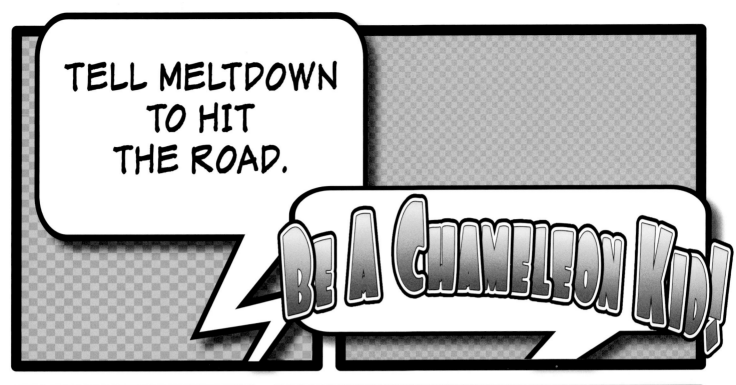

HE'LL BACK DOWN, IF YOU STAND TALL.

BE A CHAMELEON KID!

IDIOM: "STAND TALL" = BE PROUD OF YOURSELF AND CONFIDENT IN YOUR ABILITIES.

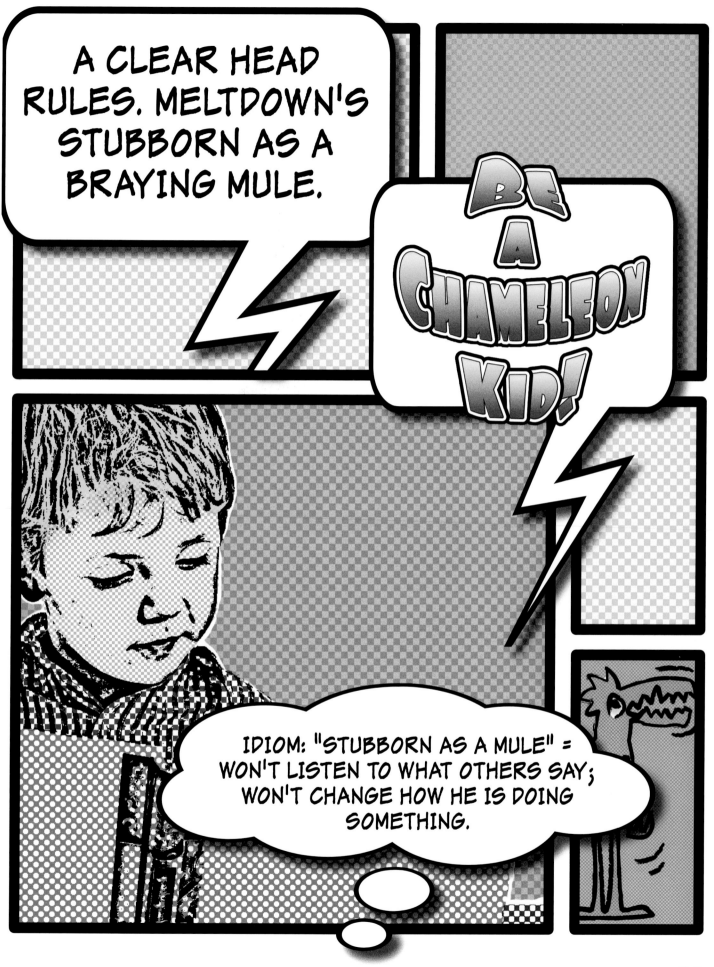

36

Be a Chameleon Kid and Take Control of Meltdown

- ☐ If you're at home or at school when Meltdown comes, go to a prearranged safe and quiet place.

- ☐ Talk with a grown-up you trust.

- ☐ Remind yourself of your strengths.

- ☐ Hum or sing funny songs.

- ☐ Count to 20, 200, or 2,000.

- ☐ Go for a walk or run, with your parents' or teacher's permission.

- ☐ Draw a picture of how you are feeling.

- ☐ Take a nap.

- ☐ Play a quiet game.

- ☐ Listen to a relaxing CD.

- ☐ Meditate: Sit quietly and breathe slowly. Think about your breath going in and going out. Push other thoughts out of your brain.

- ☐ Ask for help.

Activities to Help You Be a Chameleon Kid

Think about your last Meltdown and answer the following questions on a separate piece of paper:
1. What upset me and made Meltdown appear?
2. Did I make him go away? How?
3. Is there anything I can do differently next time to make Meltdown disappear faster?

Imagine Meltdown is in your classroom and answer these questions:
1. What upsets me at school so Meltdown shows up?
2. How can I get him to stop bugging me?
3. Where can I be safe from Meltdown at school?

Sometimes Meltdown follows you around on the playground. Write answers to these questions:
1. How does Meltdown get me in trouble on the playground?
2. How can I make him leave me alone?

Draw a picture of the meanest Meltdown you can imagine.

Meltdown's favorite place is probably your house. Answer the following questions:
1. What kinds of things upset me at home?
2. How do I feel when Meltdown appears at home?
3. Where in my house am I safe from him?
4. Who in my family helps me stop Meltdown?

Even Meltdown goes to a restaurant when he is hungry. Answer these questions:
1. What upsets me at a restaurant?
2. How can I fight Meltdown there?

Draw a picture of what goes on inside your head when you are having a Meltdown.

Draw a picture of what your body looks like, or feels like, when Meltdown comes.

Related Books by Elaine M. Larson

I Am Utterly Unique: Celebrating the Strengths of Children with Asperger Syndrome and High-Functioning Autism

Discover the unique characteristics and abilities of children with Asperger Syndrome and high-functioning autism – from A to Z. This book, laid out in an A-to-Z format, celebrates the extraordinary gifts and unique perspectives that children with ASD possess. Each page of this playful alphabet book presents one of the children's many talents and abilities. The kid-friendly illustrations and clever text create a positive portrayal of children with ASD. Designed to help children with ASD grow in self-awareness of their many capabilities, this book encourages dialogue with siblings, friends, parents and teachers. ISBN 1931282897

Elaine Marie Larson; illustrated by Vivian Strand

Code 9961 (Hardcover)   Price $18.95

The Kaleidoscope Kid: Focusing on the Strengths of Children with Asperger Syndrome and High-Functioning Autism

The Kaleidoscope Kid is written for children with Asperger Syndrome and high-functioning autism to remind them of their many special gifts and intellectual strengths. Their outlook and creative ways are truly as variable and colorful as the view through a kaleidoscope.

The reader is reminded that children with Asperger Syndrome and high-functioning autism can proudly acknowledge that they are excellent, special and one-of-a-kind individuals. They are usually truthful, helpful and dependable. The book is an enjoyable companion to Elaine Marie Larson's first book, I Am Utterly Unique, an A-B-C book on the positive traits exhibited by children on the autism spectrum, for children ages 4-10. While written for young readers, The Kaleidoscope Kid entertains and educates readers of all ages through light verse and colorful, light-hearted illustrations. ISBN 1931282412

Elaine Marie Larson; illustrated by Vivian Strand

Code 9977 (Hardcover)   Price: $17.95

Other AAPC Books for Young Readers

When My Worries Get Too Big! A Relaxation Book for Children Who Live with Anxiety

Kari Dunn Buron

Code 9962   Price $15.95

My Sensory Book: Working Together to Explore Sensory Issues and the Big Feelings They Can Cause: A Workbook for Parents, Professionals, and Children

Lauren H. Kerstein, LCSW

Code 9006   Price $21.95

Arnie and His School Tools: Simple Sensory Solutions That Build Success

Jennifer Veenendall

Code 9002   Price: $18.95

Amazingly ... Alphie! Understanding and Accepting Different Ways of Being

Roz Espin; illustrated by Beverley Ransom

Code 9927   Price: $15.95

Oliver Onion: The Onion Who Learns to Accept and Be Himself

Diane Murrell

Code 9939   Price: $16.95

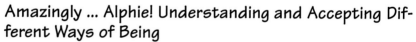

To order, visit AAPC at www.asperger.net or call toll-free 1-877-277-8254

Autism Asperger Publishing Co.
P.O. Box 23173
Shawnee Mission, Kansas 66283-0173
www.asperger.net • 913.897.1004